ANIMAL FARM

NOTES

including
- *Orwell's Life and Career*
- Animal Farm *and Anti-Utopian Fiction*
- *List of Characters*
- *Critical Commentaries*
- *Character Analyses*
- *Critical Analysis*
- *Questions for Review*
- *Selected Bibliography*

by
L. David Allen, Ph.D.
University of Nebraska
and
Frank H. Thompson, Jr., M.A.

D0111636

Cliffs Notes
INCORPORATED
LINCOLN, NEBRASKA 68501

Editor

Gary Carey, M.A.
University of Colorado

Consulting Editor

James L. Roberts, Ph.D.
Department of English
University of Nebraska

ISBN 0-8220-0174-8
© Copyright 1981
by
Cliffs Notes, Inc.
All Rights Reserved
Printed in U.S.A.

1995 Printing

Cliffs Notes, Inc.   Lincoln, Nebraska

CONTENTS

ANIMAL FARM NOTES

ORWELL'S LIFE AND CAREER

George Orwell, whose real name was Eric Blair, was born in 1903, in Bengal, India, the son of a minor official in the Indian Civil Service. As was customary, his mother brought him back to England when he was eight to be educated, along with his two sisters. Orwell was sent to a boarding school on the South Coast, a school whose students were largely sons of the wealthy. To attract such students, the school concentrated mainly on "cramming" boys for entrance to Harrow and Eton. Orwell was one of a few boys allowed to attend at a lower tuition, a practice followed to insure the winning of scholarships for the honor of the school. He came from what he himself called the "lower-upper-middle class" and hence was subjected to the snobbery of the other boys and the headmaster and his wife.

Orwell went to Eton in 1917 on a scholarship. The atmosphere was freer here, he made friends, and he read a good deal. He also encountered, for the first time, popular liberal and socialist ideas. Such ideas were common subjects of discussion at Eton, especially in the period immediately following the First World War. When he graduated in 1921, he decided not to go to a university, although he could have. Instead, he joined the Civil Service and went to Burma as a sergeant in the Indian Imperial Police.

Orwell served in Burma from 1922 to 1927. As a policeman he was, of course, the embodiment of British imperialism to the natives, a painful reversal of roles in comparison to life as a schoolboy. He intensely disliked being the instrument by which power was exercised over the Burmese; on the other hand, he had to play the part of one in authority. When he returned to England on leave in 1927, he resigned his post.

For various reasons, not all of them clear even to Orwell himself, he deliberately chose to live among working-class people in Paris and among tramps in England for more than a year. These experiences form the basis for his first book, an autobiographical work he called *Down and Out in Paris and London*, published in 1933. Although he had published some early writing under his real name, he chose the pseudonym *George Orwell* as the author of this first major work. He later explained that he took the last name from an English river near which he had once lived and he chose the first name because it was typically English. In any case, this was probably a symbolic act signaling his choice of vocation as well as his attitude toward his own country.

During these years he worked as a teacher, and after he married, he and his wife kept a village pub and a village general store. His income was small, and his first book brought him very little money. His first novel, *Burmese Days*, based on his experiences in Burma, came out in 1934. In 1935 he published another novel, *A Clergyman's Daughter*, which makes use, in part, of his teaching experiences.

Although by now he had received positive critical notice in a few places, he was not making enough income from his writing to depend on it entirely. His novel *Keep the Aspidistra Flying*, published in 1936, was based on his experiences at this time as a clerk in a bookstore. He became a socialist during this period, and when his publisher encouraged him to visit a depressed industrial area and write about his personal reactions, he took the opportunity to put his political convictions into action. The results of his trip, *The Road to Wigan Pier*, came out in 1937.

Meanwhile, the Spanish Civil War had broken out, and although Orwell went as an observer and reporter, he found himself enlisting on the Republican side. By chance, he joined a militia loyal to the P.O.U.M., a Marxist, anti-Stalinist political party, rather than the better known (at least in America at the time) International Brigade, which was ultimately Communist-controlled. He was badly wounded on the front, and by the time he recovered from his wounds, the Republican government was dominated by Communist groups responsive to direction from Russia, and the purge of other political parties, including the P.O.U.M., was under way. Orwell and his wife were forced to leave Spain for fear of imprisonment and possible execution. His experiences in the Spanish Civil War are recorded in *Homage to Catalonia*, published in 1938.

Upon his return to England, Orwell published another novel, *Coming Up for Air*, in 1939. This was the first of his books to sell well. The war which he had predicted in this book was soon under way, and although he tried to enter the army, he was rejected for service because of his health. In spite of the tuberculosis from which he suffered all his life, he was accepted in the Home Guard. During the Second World War, he worked for a time in the Indian Service of the British Broadcasting Corporation.

Two more books, collections of essays, appeared in 1940 and 1941: *Inside the Whale, and Other Essays* and *The Lion and the Unicorn: Socialism and the English Genius.* In addition, during this time, Orwell did a great deal of political writing. A regular column, "As I Please," appeared in the *London Tribune*, and he contributed to the *Observer, Manchester Evening News, Partisan Review,* and *New Leader.*

In 1945 Orwell published the first of the two books for which he is generally known, *Animal Farm;* like *Nineteen Eighty-Four,* an anti-utopian novel, it is cast in the form of a satire. The obvious subject of the satire is Soviet Russia, but more generally it has to do with totalitarianism of any kind. The success of the book, especially in this country, gave Orwell an income he had never before enjoyed.

Dickens, Dali, and Others, another collection of essays, appeared in 1946. With the death of his wife in the same year, Orwell had to assume the complete care of his adopted son. In order to find the time to complete a book which embodied the ideas that concerned him most at this time, he moved to the Scottish Hebrides. *Nineteen Eighty-Four,* his most celebrated book, was published in 1949. In it, Orwell represents a society of the near future which is a projection of certain aspects of life in the contemporary world. Although he remarried and was planning new work for the future, he died in London, in early 1950, from poor health and exhaustion.

Two other collections of essays appeared shortly after his death: *Shooting an Elephant, and Other Essays,* in 1950, and *Such, Such Were the Joys,* in 1953.

ANIMAL FARM AND ANTI-UTOPIAN FICTION

The tradition of utopian fiction—fiction predicated on the possibility of a perfect existence for man—is very old, as old as the story of the Garden of Eden in Genesis, at least for the Western world. It embodies both nostalgia for a legendary Golden Age and hope for the way man might live in some distant future.

Although *The Republic* of Plato is an older work, the name for this kind of fiction comes from Sir Thomas More's *Utopia*, published in Latin in 1516. In it, a character discovers a land called Utopia, or Nowhere Land. A popular work, it was translated into English in 1551, and it has since served as a model for writers with the same purpose. Francis Bacon's *The New Atlantis* (1626) and Jonathan Swift's *Gulliver's Travels* (1726) are further examples of utopian novels.

The nineteenth century was particularly interested in the idea of utopia, both in literature and in social experiments. In English literature there are such books as Samuel Butler's *Erewhon* (*nowhere* spelled backward) (1872) and William Morris' *News from Nowhere* (1891). Tennyson, in "Locksley Hall" (1842), writes of seeing a "vision of the world" in which finally man learns to live at peace with himself in a "federation of the world." In American literature, Edward Bellamy's *Looking Backward* (1888) and Herman Melville's *Typee* (1846) and *Omoo* (1847) are examples of the same impulse to see man in an uncorrupted state. This desire is related to the idea of the frontier in American history. The West allowed the possibility of establishing an ideal society or community free of the historical evils which man had suffered in Europe. When the peaceful community which Huckleberry Finn and his companion Jim establish on the raft is disrupted by the world, Huck eventually decides to "light out for the territory." Twain accurately reflects, in *The Adventures of Huckleberry Finn* (1885), the impulse to flee to the frontier and away from civilization. This is echoed in our own time in Holden Caulfield's desire to establish a community of the innocent somewhere in the West, in J. D. Salinger's *The Catcher in the Rye*.

Men in the nineteenth century believed in the perfectability of mankind and in the real possibility of an ultimate utopia, a time when all men would be able to live together in a united world in a state of peace. But the events of history in the twentieth century have undermined that belief. Both cold and hot wars have followed each other in quick succession; revolutions and civil wars have clouded the orderly progress of man toward some better future. Totalitarianism has become a fact that can hardly be ignored, from Hitler's Germany to the Russia of Stalin and later Soviet leaders.

The idea that man can be directed for purposes other than that of developing the best in his nature, is, of course, directly opposed to the belief in man's perfectability. In our time, there has arisen what some critics call the anti-utopian novel – a kind of fiction which shows man at the mercy of a purpose over which he has no control. Not man perfected but man perverted – this is the way the anti-utopian novel views the future. The motive for this new kind of novel may arise from the certainty that man can now destroy not only himself as an individual but all mankind, and that governments can bend people to any kind of purpose whatsoever. Usually such anti-utopian novels are intended as a criticism of the times in which the author lives, much as was the case with nineteenth-century utopian novels.

When Orwell began to write *Animal Farm* at the end of 1943, he was in a particularly uncomfortable position. He had always been convinced that the Marxist revolution of 1917 had been betrayed by Stalin; to Orwell, Stalin's character as a power-hungry assassin had been made abundantly clear. His lack of respect for truth, consistency, and moral principles had been especially underlined by his rapid propaganda shift in 1939 toward Germany, and the rapid return shift in 1941 when Germany attacked Russia. No one, however, had the courage to condemn Russia's actions in 1943 because she was fighting bravely against Germany and delaying the feared attack on England. The ironic climax of this military maneuver came at the very time Orwell was writing *Animal Farm*, when the Western Allies sat down with the Communists at the Teheran Conference in December, 1943.

Orwell's greatest fear was that people would easily forget what had happened in the immediate past; it was as if history had been rewritten, and moral principles as well. Orwell therefore wrote *Animal Farm* for an audience of the people and for leaders of Western democracy in order to remind them of the facts. His fears about Soviet Russia, which he understood even in 1943, were shown after the war to be true; immediately after the war, Russia, by her actions in taking over many eastern European countries and in refusing to cooperate with the Allies, alienated the West, ending the temporary anti-Nazi alliance, and retired behind the "Iron Curtain." In an introduction to a foreign-language edition of *Animal Farm*, Orwell says his main intention was to show how false the popular idea was that Soviet Russia was a socialist state: he wanted to save socialism from communism.

The anti-utopian novel is a specialized branch of fiction, like the novel of ideas, for instance. And it is true that the author of such a novel is mainly concerned with depicting a certain kind of society. But since he is writing a novel, by necessity he must use certain means available to any novelist: plot, setting, characterization, point of view, structure, and the like. To say that he bends these formal aspects to his purpose is only to describe what any good novelist does. The success with which he makes the reader accept the reality he has created is the only meaningful test of his ability as a writer. Orwell, after all, had written several novels before he produced either *Animal Farm* or *Nineteen Eighty-Four*. By the time of these later books, he was no longer satisfied with the novel as he had written it, and he turned to the anti-utopian novel as the most effective means to embody his urgent purposes.

LIST OF CHARACTERS

Old Major

The venerable old boar whose vision of a better life and his call for rebellion are the inspiration for the founding of Animal Farm.

Snowball

A young boar whose persuasive powers of speech and theoretical intelligence make him a contender for the leadership of Animal Farm.

Napoleon

Another young boar whose ambition and direct approach to gaining power cause him to win the struggle for leadership of Animal Farm.

Boxer

A cart horse of immense strength, great loyalty, and small intelligence who is foremost in the projects requiring physical labor.

Clover

A mare whose motherly concern for Boxer and the other animals makes her a source of personal strength for all, especially during difficult times in the history of Animal Farm.

Benjamin

A donkey whose skepticism about any kind of society and about human nature persists unchanged.

Moses

A raven who regales the animals with stories about the better life to come on Sugarcandy Mountain.

Mollie

A mare whose frivolous attitude and personal vanity eventually cause her to leave Animal Farm and go to work for the owner of a pub.

Squealer

A porker who is used by Napoleon to explain away the actions of the pigs that appear contrary to the Commandments, on which Animal Farm is founded.

Mr. Jones

The human owner of Manor Farm; he is driven from his property by the animals.

Mr. Frederick

A neighboring farmer who is a shrewd businessman and who runs an efficient farming operation.

Mr. Pilkington

Another neighboring farmer; he neglects his farm and spends most of his time hunting and fishing.

Mr. Whymper

An insignificant local solicitor who acts as the agent between Napoleon and the human beings he trades with.

CRITICAL COMMENTARIES

CHAPTER I

Much of the effect of the novel, its direct impact, depends upon Orwell's management of point of view. The story is told by an impersonal narrator who is separate from the action of the story; he presents the events from the perspective of the "average citizens" of Animal Farm. That is to say, the reader is never allowed to view events as, say, Napoleon or Snowball (two boars) see them; indeed, the reader is only rarely allowed to view events directly from the perspective of one particular animal. This impersonality is, of course, essential to maintaining the plausibility of the novel.

The choice of point of view has several consequences. It keeps the human beings who do appear in the story as far as possible in the background. It encourages the reader to believe, for the purposes of the story, that the animals do act as they are shown to. It makes it possible for Orwell to show the good will and hopes of the ordinary animals slowly undermined and destroyed by the selfish machinations of the pigs. In short, it is exactly the right point of view from which to present the novel most effectively.

Just as the point of view is established immediately, in the second paragraph of the novel, so also are the characters quickly drawn for the reader. It is more or less true that in a novel of this sort, character change is less important than in the conventional work of fiction. But to say that the characters do not change at all but are only more fully revealed by the end is to play fast and loose with the usual, formal aspects of the novel. Boxer, who is still repeating his maxim about working harder before he dies, is not quite the same at the end of the novel as he is at the beginning. He can no longer really be as optimistic as he once was. Although he chooses to ignore the evidence that the animals are becoming worse off each year, he senses that his dreams are *not* coming true. Maybe this seems like little change, but how much more is the ordinary fictional character shown to change in his lifetime?

The animals are just animal enough and just human enough to be believable. Roughly, their actions are characteristic of animals; their ideas and words, of human beings. Were Orwell to have forgotten this concept of character for his novel, what happens would not have the plausibility it does. The way in which Boxer and Clover walk into the barn among the other animals who are coming to the meeting which has been called by Old Major, and the way the cat looks after her own comfort, are but two instances of fidelity to animal behavior.

Obviously, Old Major's speech in the barn is a signal that the reader is to expect the animals to talk and think like human beings. Old Major is an elder statesman and a visionary, and he presents his vision in a step-by-step fashion well suited to his audience. That is, he begins by sketching in the unhappy lot of animals in England and by suggesting that England could support many more animals and provide them a much better life if it were not for Man. He describes for the farm animals many instances of Man's cruelty to animals, and he tells them that he envisions a future happy time in which Man has been removed, although the animals must be careful not to listen to Man's false and misleading arguments if this future is to come to pass in some unspecified time. Even the vote on whether or not to include the rats as "brothers" supports his ideal of the brotherhood of all animals. He even lists the things – the vices – that are Man's and which the animals must avoid if this future free state is to be achieved. It is out of this speech that the ideals of Animal Farm are conceived, as well as the principles under which it will be operated.

Old Major's view of life is simple: man is bad; animals are good. His vision for the future of the animals is also simple: it is nostalgic and pastoral, as is shown in the song *Beasts of England*, to which the animals respond enthusiastically and sing five times in succession, waking Mr. Jones, their master, from his drunken sleep. Both Old Major's view of life and his vision of the future are, as the reader quickly sees, oversimplified. Old Major's visionary ideals are the strength of Animal Farm in the beginning, but they become its major weakness as time goes on. For the purpose of Orwell's satire, however, everything in the novel grows out of the views and the vision presented in this speech.

On the level of plot, everything that happens also comes as a result of Old Major's speech. Expecting the rebellion to come in some indefinable time in the future, the animals are not prepared for having the freedom Old Major envisions. They are easily led by whoever is ambitious enough to assume leadership. And they are likewise easily led to believe that everything that occurs is done in their behalf, although soon this is not so. Old Major's vision has such a lasting effect that finally the animals begin acting against their own welfare. They realize too late that they have been duped, as of course they had always been, in a sense, by human beings.

The structure of the novel rises slowly, then slowly diminishes. Or it might be described as a circle, except that the animals are really not back to the point at which they started by the end of the story. Whereas under Jones they were victims, here they unwittingly become the cause of their own undoing.

Orwell's theme is the revolution betrayed – or man creating a world in which his humanity and individuality are forgotten or subverted. Having seen such a world, in fact, in Spain, Orwell represents man's inhumanity to man – using creatures against their own welfare – in both this novel and in *Nineteen Eighty-Four*. In the latter novel, he dropped the device of animal satire and presented his views more directly. In all anti-utopian novels, man goes from bad to worse.

It is of course true on one level, at least, that in *Animal Farm* Orwell has a historical theme: how the Russian revolution became not a dictatorship of the proletariat which would eventually wither away (to use the words of Marx), but simply a dictatorship, or perhaps more accurately, an oligarchy.

CHAPTER II

The physical location of Manor Farm is shown to be an ideal setting for a utopian community: it is a pleasant place to look at, it is isolated from outside interferences, and it is suitable for establishing the kind of pastoral life which Old Major dreams of. Its transformation into Animal Farm goes smoothly at first. On the other hand, the fact that it is almost an ideal setting will make even more ironic and disheartening the reality of the way in which the dream is undermined. What begins as utopia will end as the reverse.

The Rebellion, of course, comes unexpectedly, and the animals react spontaneously to the situation throughout this chapter. When the animals break into a storage shed and begin to eat their fill after Jones and his men have left them unfed for over a day, Jones and his hired hands try to beat them back with whips. This time, however, the animals become angry at this mistreatment; they turn on the humans and drive them off the farm, locking the gate against their return. Their celebratory gallop around the perimeters of the farm and their burning in a great bonfire the implements symbolizing Man's tyranny are spontaneous and emotional. Even their tour of the house—which they leave untouched, except for burying some hams and destroying the beer barrel, and which they decide should be preserved as a museum—provides them with a sense of what they have accomplished, even though they take this tour rather reluctantly. The change in the animals' situation is proclaimed for all to see when the name of the farm is changed from Manor Farm to Animal Farm and when the Seven Commandments of Animalism are painted in large letters on the barn; all the animals fully approve of these actions, cheering the pigs on as they make these changes.

The differences among the animals which distinguish them and which make possible the direction the plot takes are vividly shown. Obviously, Snowball and Napoleon will be the leaders of Animal Farm; even before the Rebellion they have set to work planning for the time when it will occur. There is a kind of unthinking acquiescence to their natural abilities on the part of the other animals. But the different temperaments and views of life of Snowball and Napoleon—shown, for example, in the way Snowball corrects Mollie's mistaken ideas during the discussion of Animalism and the way Napoleon handles the disposition of the milk—predict a rivalry between the two which, as it turns out, will cause the other animals to suffer.

Boxer and Clover are faithful party rank-and-file at the beginning of the Revolution; they have the virtue of unswerving loyalty. The other animals are a mixed lot, from Squealer, who will be used by Napoleon, to Benjamin, the perpetual skeptic.

For the reader, one of the great temptations is to read the story solely as a satire on Russian history. True enough: Snowball does represent Trotsky; Napoleon, Stalin; Moses, organized religion; and so on. But to see nothing more in the animals' characters or in their actions than this is to deprive Orwell's book of its far-reaching effect. Animal Farm is a metaphor for any society in which men of goodwill attempt to make a better life for themselves only to discover that the old evils of selfishness, pride, and hypocrisy have not been eliminated.

Good satire, in other words, is always timely; it always has specific weaknesses or evils to attack and expose, but the best satire is also timeless. It deals not merely with man in time but with the human condition in *any* time. There are Napoleons and Boxers in every society. If the satirist warns man against being corrupted by himself or others, he also makes clear that man really hasn't changed much throughout history.

A good idea, in human hands, easily becomes an evil idea. Irony goes hand in hand with satire, it is one of its means, and nothing perhaps is more ironical than Old Major's well-intentioned speech before he dies, in Chapter One. The revered leader is giving his final wisdom to the animals, and the vision he depicts of a better life is persuasive and *ought* to be true. But in his words, as the reader can see, lies the possibility for just the opposite of the good life he speaks of. To begin with, his view of human nature is unrealistic; it is the very kind of view that someone is likely to exploit. And he who exploits it will know that he can do so in the name of Old Major's wisdom, while at the same time he is building an empire for himself. Yet the maxims that come from Old Major's lips become the principles by which, for a time, the animals build their utopia and by which they themselves are subsequently undone. Old Major's view of human nature is also oversimplified. He envisions a society founded on the essential belief that man is the *sole* cause of the animals' misery, their only evil. Such a belief can easily be manipulated for selfish ends because it is an unrealistic view of human nature.

The Seven Commandments, which are to be the "unalterable laws" by which the animals live, are all predicated upon the simplified belief that man is evil, except perhaps the last Commandment. When the threat of man has been removed, it is possible that he who has selfish aims to promote can also pervert both the spirit and letter of these Commandments. What is taken in good faith, in one way, can become something else — as this novel demonstrates; it can become the means by which the animals are enslaved again.

It is ironical too that from the start the animals accept the pigs so readily as their leaders. The pigs are never said to be better than the other animals; they are only smarter or cleverer. The value of intelligence, in a social sense, at least, depends on the motives underlying its use. These motives the animals never question; much to their dismay, they are to learn later that they were terribly wrong to be so passively persuaded by the pigs' rhetoric.

The scene of the Rebellion is as ironical as other things in the story. The animals do not intend to start a rebellion; they are only hungry, having suffered from the neglect of Jones and his men. Orwell presents this scene in only two paragraphs, partly to emphasize the accidental way in which the new society starts. It also contrasts sharply with the way in which later, more important scenes are shown: for example, the Battle of the Cowshed and the Battle of the Windmill. This is a scene about which the reader should ask: but what if the animals had been fed in time? As a political parallel, historical necessity, to use the appropriate Marxist term, is really historical accident, to Orwell.

What has been but a dream and a hope for Old Major quickly becomes a philosophy called Animalism, worked out exclusively by Snowball, Napoleon, and Squealer. It is of course a parallel, in Orwell's satire, with Marxism. The name given to the set of doctrines, later embodied in the Seven Commandments, is itself revealing. Orwell's sure critical sense of propaganda is apparent here. It is a name designed to rouse "national" pride, to encourage a sense of exclusiveness. It is also a name that reveals an essential fact about Animal Farm: the term is based on a fear of man as the ever-present enemy. Animalism is akin, in this respect, to Marxism: the latter constantly raises the specter of capitalism, often in almost cartoon form. Several times in the novel, all Squealer has to do in order to bend the animals to some impossible task again is to ask if they want Jones back as their master. Animalism is clearly propaganda, not a philosophy.

CHAPTER III

The Revolution occurred in March; now it is harvest time, and the animals realize that they must take over the day-to-day operation of the farm at once. Under the supervision of the pigs, they finish the harvest in two fewer days than Jones ever had, and, in addition, they are even more thorough. As a result, food is plentiful, and life is good. In addition, under Snowball's leadership, the animals very quickly take on the characteristics of "civilized" human society. On Sundays, they hold meetings to plan the next week's work and to discuss any resolutions — all of which are proposed by the pigs, since none of the other animals can think of any to propose — and vote on them. Through such events Orwell foreshadows much of what is to come. Before long, all of the animals will simply be taking orders, much as they did from Jones, and, eventually, they will not even be voting. Snowball and Napoleon continually disagree, as their different temperaments would lead the reader to expect them to. A real struggle for power is beginning here, and it will soon be a short matter of time before one deposes the other. Who will win this struggle is clear enough from the hints Orwell has dropped so far.

Snowball is very active in forming committees, the purpose of which is to improve conditions and to improve the animals themselves. Napoleon has nothing to do with such activities; indeed, he makes his disapproval of them very clear, and he does what he can to undermine them. The animals are unable to manage committee organization, but, to a greater or lesser extent, they do learn to read and write. They are the *masses*, ready to vote but unable to understand what they are voting for or against. The disposition of the milk earlier, and now the apples, foreshadow the increasing privileges which the pigs are taking — in every way making themselves into a ruling class. Even Napoleon's taking the puppies under his personal care is ominous. It is, of course, Squealer who is the propagandist for the pigs, justifying their every action and making it seem as though the pigs are being purely altruistic. His constantly raising the threat that Jones will return is the one thing that consistently and almost universally motivates the animals; it is a great help to him in his task.

What is being shown here, in Orwell's satire, is the struggle for power. Partly, of course, it parallels the struggle between Trotsky and Stalin after the death of Lenin. But more generally, it is the struggle that occurs in any society in which the people at large really have no voice. This is shown, in one form, in Snowball's simplification of the Seven Commandments into one slogan: "Four legs good, two legs bad." The sheep are especially satisfied with this reduction of doctrine and are given to chanting it. It is just the kind of slogan which is easy to understand, dangerously simple, and flexible enough to manipulate for those who mean to hold power.

It serves Orwell's purposes to use a number of symbols throughout the story. In Chapter II, for instance, the farmhouse in which Jones lived and through which, after the Rebellion, the animals walk in awe represents to the animals all the evil that is man. It has beds and whiskey and other things which Old Major enjoined his fellow animals to abhor. It becomes significant later, then, that it is the *pigs* who move into the farmhouse. It is an early sign of their slowly assuming the role of Jones. Whips, of course, are a symbol of the animals' oppression by man, and they are among the first manmade things destroyed after the Rebellion. When, at the end of the story, Napoleon walks on two legs, the animals are not nearly so terrified of this as they are of the whip he carries. Oppression, like the kind of repression which Jones engaged in, has returned.

In the present chapter, the flag which Snowball devises and hoists every week symbolizes the animals' hopes. Later in the story when, in effect, the pigs become human beings, it is important to note that Napoleon says that he will remove the shapes on the flag which signify the animals—the hoof and horn—to pacify the human societies with whom he seeks status. The song which the animals are fond of singing, *Beasts of England*, is of course a backward-looking one, as has been pointed out before, and it is later changed under the regime of Napoleon in exchange for one that is more flattering of him.

All the symbols in the story are part of the mechanics of the satire which Orwell constructed. Like irony, symbolism is an effective means by which to criticize and to ridicule, and at the same time it carries part of the meaning of the story.

Although the structure of the novel is still in the rising stage, everywhere is seen the genesis of the elements by which the falling stage will inevitably be reached. Primarily, this is to be seen in the actions of the pigs, who are beginning to entrench themselves as leaders. The fall will neither begin nor accelerate until Napoleon has gotten rid of Snowball, an idealist who genuinely has the good of all animals as his aim for leadership. Once that is accomplished, the second half of the structure will be under way.

CHAPTER IV

Propaganda is used openly in this chapter: from Animal Farm, at the instigation of Snowball and Napoleon, there is an effort made to try to persuade the animals on other farms to join with them in the spirit of rebellion against the tyranny of their masters; and there is also the propaganda from the neighboring farmers, Frederick and Pilkington, to try to discredit the new society of Animal Farm by circulating rumors of immoral excesses in the animals' behavior and their gross failures to govern themselves.

The Battle of the Cowshed, to which the propaganda war is but a preliminary, is described in much greater detail than the Rebellion. The animals are prepared for such an attack, for Snowball has wisely studied the strategies of Caesar. Thus, when the pigeons bring word of the advancing mob of humans, the animals quickly take their places for defense. With Snowball in the forefront of the fighting, the animals lure the humans into a trap and quickly rout them. After the victory, the animals bury their one casualty, a valiant sheep, with honors. They also create two kinds of honors for those who fought—"Animal Hero, First Class" for Boxer and Snowball, and "Animal Hero, Second Class" for the dead sheep. They also name the battle after the location of the ambush, and they decide to commemorate both this battle and the Rebellion by having two ceremonies each year, during which Jones' gun will be fired on each occasion.

Orwell's purpose in using this scene is, of course, different from his intention in so briefly presenting the first attack of the animals on human beings. The animals' strategy in the Battle of the Cowshed has been planned in advance, and the animals perform like a disciplined army, heedless of their personal safety. They are still in the revolutionary stage in which they feel a sense of their own existence as a community.

But Orwell also has another purpose. Later in the story, when Snowball has been driven from Animal Farm by Napoleon, the latter uses these events of the Battle of the Cowshed to accuse his adversary of deception and cowardice. Snowball's actions in the battle are such that they can be viewed quite differently by Napoleon later, although at this time Snowball is acclaimed a hero and is decorated.

The farm of Foxwood, in part, represents England; the farm of Pinchfield represents Germany. But Orwell means to say more than this, of course. As elsewhere, he is satirizing the actions of any nations who see an opportunity for self-aggrandizement in a neighboring country. After all, men from both Foxwood and Pinchfield help Jones in his attempt to "liberate," to restore law and order to Animal Farm. They are obviously more concerned, of course, with what they can get from the situation than what Jones can reclaim.

As critics have often pointed out, *Animal Farm* is effective partly because of the convincing details which Orwell includes—for example, the naming of the battle by the inhabitants of Animal Farm, and the giving of decorations and the establishing of days to celebrate the animals' victories. These parallels have direct reference to Russia, but they are the kinds of details which are persuasive no matter what specific society Orwell had under his critical eye.

Irony as a means by which the satire is effected is often used. The irony of the animals defending themselves at the Battle of the Cowshed, at the risk of losing their own lives, for a society in which power has never been theirs and never really will be, is the main means by which Orwell carries out his satirical purposes. The irony, in this case, does not lead to humor, as it sometimes does, but rather to an awareness that man does not often know what he does, but yet he feels that he must act. Like any human being, the animals go into battle with the best of intentions; only later do they realize that they have been duped. Then it is too late. There are, of course, other instances in this chapter of the way in which irony functions as a part of the machinery of satire. Clearly, irony can be used in fiction for other than satirical purposes.

CHAPTER V

The scene in which Napoleon takes over the exclusive leadership of Animal Farm is preceded by a period of time during which Mollie, Jones' cart horse, defects in order to once again have the sugar cubes, the attention, and the pretty ribbons she so dearly loves; in addition, during this time, the animals are divided over several issues. The building of the windmill and the defense of the farm are the two subjects at the core of the struggle taking place. When the climactic Sunday meeting is held, factions have formed on either side regarding the question of the windmill. The rival leaders act as the reader expects them to. Snowball is persuasive, picturing the windmill as a means of providing many benefits for all of the animals. Napoleon says little, but just when it seems as though Snowball's persuasive arguments have won the day, Napoleon summons his dogs – which he has kept hidden – and successfully puts an end to the threat of power from Snowball, who barely escapes through a hedge with his life.

The speed with which Napoleon takes matters into his own hands shows the great care which he has taken to prepare for this moment. As in all such coups, the combination of his planning and the animals' surprise enables him to seize power with almost no resistance at all. His well-worked out plans – first, the abolition of the Sunday debates and the communal planning of the work, and later the decision to build the windmill – strengthen his position. The follow-up propagandizing and the revision of history, in the course of which it is claimed that Snowball was an enemy all along and that the plans for the windmill were originally Napoleon's, enable Napoleon to take over complete charge of Animal Farm; already several parallels between him and Mr. Jones are evident.

What has happened, although the animals do not realize this until much later, is the establishment of a dictatorship. The use of personal bodyguards (the nine ferocious dogs) here is one of the first signs. Another is the change of routine: for example, abolishing the open meeting for debates every Sunday morning and establishing in its place an assembly during which the animals are given *orders* for the week to come. Yet another change is the disinterring of the skull of Old Major, to be used as an object of veneration by all the animals. Finally, Snowball, the rival to leadership, is discredited with fabricated evidence and specious arguments that he was an enemy all along.

On one level, Orwell is alluding, in his satire, to Stalin's assumption of power in Russia. But the historical parallel depicted here can also be understood in more general terms. It is the way in which any people are deceived when an unscrupulous individual is bent on using them, manipulating them for his own purposes. As in all such instances, what *appears* to be and what *is* are quite contradictory things. The disagreements between Snowball and Napoleon, for instance, are used by the latter at the right time to attempt to seize power. The masses—the animals—are privy to none of this and are not even sure they are being used when the moment comes. Napoleon's takeover of Animal Farm is a clear sign that events are moving to the stage of falling after a rise to a kind of peak. The windmill, for example, was proposed by Snowball as a pinnacle of success for the community of Animal Farm. True, the windmill will be built and rebuilt, but for different reasons. Small details also show the way in which events will revert to being very much like they were in the beginning or perhaps worse. The dogs act toward Napoleon as they acted toward Jones or would act toward any human being. Of course, the fact that the animals cannot discern the foreshadowings of their fate under Napoleon continues to be one of the major ironies of the novel.

CHAPTER VI

Orwell's use of point of view enables him to show very effectively the way in which the regime of Napoleon affects the animals on the farm. Since they are no longer allowed to participate in making any decisions about their lives, their reactions have to do mainly with their personal comfort or discomfort and their measuring their present lot against what they remember of the past. Their life is hard: they put in sixty-hour weeks until Napoleon calls for "voluntary" work on Sunday afternoons (the alternative is losing half their rations). Work on the windmill proceeds slowly, taking time away from the other tasks of the farm, so that the second year is not as successful as the first was. Still, the animals believe that life is better than it was under Jones.

Thus, the animals continue to work hard, although only a few are as willing to continue to accept every edict from Napoleon in the way Boxer does, as he leads the workers by example, straining himself to the limit and putting in as much volunteer time as he can. On the other hand, none are as skeptical as Benjamin. It is mainly a matter of their accepting, more or less, what comes along, although some are puzzled that the past is made to seem different from what they remember—for example, the change in the Commandment forbidding any animal to sleep in a bed. Always they are faced with the choice, usually put forth by Squealer, of accepting Napoleon's leadership or allowing Jones to take over again. Thus, they make the only choice possible to them—Napoleon's choice, or more properly put, his edict.

As with all dictators, Napoleon establishes a personal style of life to which everything in the community must contribute. His need to make the governed respond constantly dictates most of what Napoleon does: he establishes trade with humans and actually allows a human onto the grounds of the farm (although the animals fear Mr. Whymper, they are cheered by the sight of Napoleon giving him orders); the pigs also move into the house and sleep in beds; they continually insist that the windmill be built and rebuilt, and they encourage the use of titles when others address Napoleon. He is their "Leader." Like his satirical parallel, Stalin, Napoleon makes every facet of life into a matter of state.

One object of Orwell's satire, the revision of the past to make it conform to the present, as in the case of the decision to trade with human beings, was of particular importance to Orwell. He came back to it again, in greater detail, in *Nineteen Eighty-Four*. The past, after all, exists only as it is remembered or recorded. To be in the position to rewrite history is to control both the past and the future. Throughout this novel, the Seven Commandments are revised, one by one, to rationalize what Napoleon decides to do. Having no source for these Commandments but the wall of the barn, the animals are forced to accept the changes as they are mysteriously made because, sadly, none of them bothered to learn to read well.

The two-year plan for the building of the windmill, and subsequent plans, are, of course, reminiscent of Stalin's Five-Year Plans. They were the dictator's means of keeping the masses engaged on such laborious and lengthy projects that they had little time to think and were given constant occasions, under the pressure of propaganda, to perform heroically. As a parallel, when the half-finished windmill is blown down in a severe November windstorm, Napoleon exhorts them to work even harder to rebuild it. He also proclaims that Snowball is responsible for the disaster, and he promises rewards for any animal who captures Snowball. This scapegoat serves to keep the animals in perpetual fear of an enemy who may undo them at any moment. Only Napoleon, the all-powerful leader, can save them from the enemy, the imaginary figure which the leader himself created.

It is all a part of Napoleon's plan to create a reality in Animal Farm to correspond to his wishes. This is, and must be, an integral part of any totalitarian system. It must not merely be better than any other society; it must also be different. This serves to increase the isolation in which the society exists. The greater the isolation, the easier it is for the omnipotent leader to maintain his godlike stature. This is part of Orwell's theme in the novel: man no longer exists as an individual; only the leader exists as a separate entity, and the masses are but extensions of him.

Like other symbols in the novel, the farmhouse and the windmill, for example, are used to support the satire and to serve as the means for conveying the theme of the novel. The farmhouse symbolizes *man*, with all of the evils and inequities connected with him. When the pigs decide to live in the farmhouse—Napoleon does this to satisfy a whim now that he has the seat of power—their eventual identity with Jones and other human beings is foreshadowed. For Snowball, the windmill was a sign of the enlightened progress for which the community of Animal Farm was founded. For Napoleon, it is a means by which the animals can be kept busy indefinitely. To the animals, it is a barely understood symbol of the better life to which they all aspire.

CHAPTER VII

Like Stalin, and like any dictator, Napoleon must make it appear as though everything is going well under his rule. Thus, even though the winter has been hard and supplies are running low, he makes it appear that Animal Farm has more supplies than it needs, so that Whymper's reports in Willingdon will counteract the rumors that Animal Farm's economy is about to collapse. In addition, Napoleon also arranges to sell eggs in order to buy the supplies necessary to survive until spring.

Like Stalin, and like any dictator, Napoleon cannot allow any threat to his power. Thus, when the hens rebel at the number of eggs that will be taken from them, Napoleon orders that their rations be cut off completely, and his dogs enforce the order. Furthermore, when other things begin to go wrong, the specter of Snowball sabotaging their efforts and the threat of Jones returning are brought forth with increasing frequency to keep the animals in line.

Like Stalin, and like any dictator, Napoleon must prove his power by making others suffer; hence, Napoleon's purge, like those in Russia in the mid-1930s. Under the pretext of a rebellious attitude, four pigs are made to confess and are executed. Even Boxer, who had roused Squealer's wrath by arguing about Snowball's initial intentions, might have been one of the victims had he not been large enough to catch a dog in mid-air and pin it to the ground. The confession of the pigs and Napoleon's call for the truth sets off a wave of hysterical confessions of guilt and immediate executions. The only reason for this, as in any other dictatorship, is to make power visible, to make it felt and feared.

The animals are shocked by this bloody spectacle, but the environment is such now that Boxer's determination to work harder, although he doesn't understand the events that have occurred, is typical of the attitude of most of the animals. There is little else they can do. Napoleon, at this stage, is becoming more and more eccentric. He appears only with due ceremony and only when he is surrounded by his bodyguard of vicious dogs. He makes himself inaccessible: the more power he acquires and exercises, the more mysterious he becomes. A "god," after all, cannot mingle too often with his devotees, else the latter may find reason not to believe in his omnipotence.

The animals' gathering on the knoll is an intended parallel, in the structure of the novel, with the first time the animals gathered there and looked upon their own land, just after the Rebellion. Clover tries to recall the time of the Rebellion, when hopes were high, and she is sad to feel that they have not achieved what they set out to do. The purges are wrong, she feels, but her conclusion does not mean that she will be disobedient to Napoleon in the future.

The banning of *Beasts of England* seems designed to cut the animals off from the earlier vision, the one that gave rise to the creation of Animal Farm. The new anthem is less nostalgic and more nationalistic. Later, the official poet, Minimus, will produce works extolling the almost sacred qualities of their leader, Napoleon. Like all official "new" anthems, this one is largely ignored by the animals; what moves them, and comforts them, is the old one, so closely associated with the Rebellion. It continues to have an underground life in spite of official pronouncements against it by Napoleon.

CHAPTER VIII

Napoleon's systematic lying is, of course, apparent to the reader but not to the animals. Thus, although the animals are working long hours and harder than ever before, Squealer presents long lists of figures to prove that things are better than they ever have been before. The animals accept this idea in spite of the fact that the animals are often hungry. More commandments are rewritten to justify, after the fact, the actions Napoleon takes—such things as having separate apartments, eating from the best dishes, requiring public celebration of his birthday, adding new titles for himself, taking all the praise for what the other animals produce, displaying his picture, and drinking whiskey. Not even finding Squealer in circumstances making it absolutely clear that he is the one who changes the Commandments on the barn causes the animals to question anything they are told.

The discrediting of Snowball continues, as it must in order to enhance Napoleon's "image," as in the last chapter; the attempts to blacken his character so completely raises minor doubts in the minds of only a few of the animals, but it does not cause them to question what they are told. The negotiations with the neighboring farms of Foxwood and Pinchfield are transparent attempts by Napoleon to play one farmer against another, but they are obvious only to the reader. One lie succeeds another lie, with Squealer sent out to pacify the animals whenever there are outrages or questions about the acts practiced by Napoleon.

The Battle of the Windmill is quite another matter from the Battle of the Cowshed or the Rebellion itself. This latest battle is another sign in the structure of the novel that the plot is nearing its climax. The battle takes place several days after Napoleon has sold the timber to Frederick of Pinchfield Farm. Frederick cheated Napoleon with forged notes, and now Frederick intends to take over Animal Farm. He and his men come prepared. They drive the animals back with their guns, take possession of the large pasture, and use blasting powder to destroy the windmill. Despair replaces surprise and hope, but the destruction of the windmill so enrages the animals that they disregard the guns and eventually drive the invaders away. In spite of the fact that Napoleon proclaims a great victory and orders several days of celebrations and state funerals, this event and the recent purges are further steps in the shattering of the animals' hopes. Still, Old Major's vision of the good life so persists that most of the animals are unwilling or unable to see Animal Farm as anything but a utopia for them, even though they do not have as much to eat now as during the time when Jones owned the farm.

Propaganda and its uses are, of course, one of the major targets of criticism in Orwell's satire. Several good examples are used in this chapter. The titles which Napoleon assumes, for which he is himself obviously the inventor, are propaganda which seems to impress only his fellow pigs. Likewise, the poem dedicated to Napoleon is so much a part of a propaganda effort that many animals do not take it very seriously. Its fulsome praise of the great leader is too tasteless even for the dullest of the animals on the farm.

In a dictatorship, the manipulation of thought and belief must be constant. Human nature, if left alone, will react to hollow-sounding words in the way Benjamin does. But Napoleon, like all dictators, must make his power constantly felt by every animal. He does so, very skillfully.

CHAPTER IX

Squealer is the apologist, the head of propaganda for Napoleon. It is his job to explain the shifts in Napoleon's policies in such a way that the animals can accept them even if they are unable to understand them. He is given almost no personality beyond that which is necessary to establish his role in the story. As a psychologist of mass behavior, he knows that the most potent argument, when all else fails, is raising the possibility that Jones might return. This and the long lists of statistics on crops are two ways in which Orwell carries out this part of his satire on Soviet society. As chief of propaganda, Squealer must also rewrite history day by day. This is done partly by rationalizing speeches, in which gray or black becomes white, but also by altering the Commandments on the barn to conform to whatever Napoleon wants to do at the moment. After Napoleon is firmly entrenched as leader, he seldom appears in person to the animals; instead, he sends Squealer with the latest inflated statistics or the latest orders.

Thus, life continues to be hard, and rations are again reduced for the working animals. Squealer, however, convinces them once again that it is only right that the pigs should have more because of the nature of the work they do. He even convinces them that strict equality in such things as rations is *not* good for them and is opposed to the true principles of Animalism. When the young pigs are born, Napoleon announces that the animals will build a school for them, adding to all the other work which the animals do. Elitism is fostered when the young pigs are encouraged to keep to themselves and when the other animals are told that they must step aside whenever they meet a pig. The pigs also begin wearing green ribbons on their tails on Sundays, and they begin brewing their own beer, appropriating all the barley grown on the farm for themselves. In order to distract the animals' attention from these things and such other things as Napoleon's having himself elected as president of the new Republic which he has proclaimed, parades, songs, and speeches become more frequent, and "spontaneous" demonstrations in honor of Napoleon are encouraged; in fact, however, they are made mandatory. The animals grumble a little, but they accept it all.

The animals cannot understand why Moses, the raven, is allowed to return and remain on the farm. The reader can see, of course, exactly why he is tolerated. So long as the animals listen to his tales of Sugarcandy Mountain, where an afterlife is better, they will think and complain less often about the hard life they are enduring. Napoleon is here using the argument of Marx, who thought of religion as being an opiate of the people. Moses is harmless so long as he doesn't interfere with Napoleon's plans for the animals.

One of the many ironies in the novel is the way in which Boxer is used by the pigs and is then discarded when he is no longer able to work. Boxer is, above all, loyal, and he is devoted to hard work—even though he is bothered a great deal by the wounds which he received in the Battle of the Windmill; he daily pushes himself to get more and more done. He tries to do whatever Napoleon says to do, and thus he is admired by the other animals and is praised by Napoleon.

But the reader can see that Orwell intends to show the difference between Boxer's idea of himself and the role which he plays for Napoleon as only one more cog in the machine called Animal Farm. Thus, when Boxer's lungs give out late in the summer, the pigs appear solicitous and tell the other animals that he will be sent to the veterinary clinic for treatment. The animals are therefore understandably shocked when they realize that Boxer has been sold by the pigs to the glue factory; what they don't realize at the time is that he has been "used" all along. And, of course, Squealer is immediately on the defense, counteracting rumors and convincing the animals that Boxer died in great comfort and dignity; the idea that Boxer was sold to the "knacker" is simply a misunderstanding.

Boxer's position is important because, in many ways, he represents the masses who live at Animal Farm. None of the animals other than the pigs really know until the very end of the novel that Animal Farm is really Manor Farm with a new name. Because they still believe in Old Major's vision, they are easy prey for such an individual of unscrupulous ambition like Napoleon.

Many things signal the fact that the structure of the novel has reached the stage of rapid fall. Certainly Napoleon's having himself elected president of the Republic of Animal Farm is one. Certainly Napoleon's keeping the young pigs apart from the other animals, in both education and normal social contact, is another. He is making Animal Farm into a class society with two groups: the ruling class, with privileges and honors; and the workers, with the privilege of performing their jobs without complaint and without reward. Napoleon is becoming more and more like Jones all the time.

CHAPTER X

It is especially clear at the end of the novel why Orwell chose the point of view he did. Throughout the story the readers understands what the animals do not because they have the advantage of a greater range of vision. The animals understand only so much as they are able to see; this in itself is a demonstration of why they allow Napoleon to work against their welfare. Their discovery of the truth about the society of Animal Farm, in the scene in which they watch the pigs and the human beings together in the farmhouse, is made to seem very real, and it affects the readers in spite of their superior knowledge. Orwell is convincing: the animals really are full of good will but they are deceived and sold out. The logic of the plot requires that human beings appear at the end of the novel. They provide the circumstances in which it is shown that Napoleon has become indistinguishable from Jones. That is, over the years between the events in Chapter IX and Chapter X, the pigs have taken on more and more characteristics of human beings: they have finally begun walking upright and carrying whips (much to the fright of the animals), they subscribe to newspapers and magazines, they have a telephone, and they dress in human clothes. In the meantime, all of the Commandments have been changed and modified and finally replaced by the Commandment that proclaims that all animals are equal but some animals are *more* equal than others.

The farm has prospered. New fields have been added, and the windmill brings in a handsome profit. The animals, however, have none of the things envisioned by either Old Major or Snowball, and life is hard and meager for them; nevertheless, the few animals remaining from the time of the Rebellion and the new recruits, who have been chosen for their ability to work rather than for their intelligence, believe that they are free and thus have dignity. They do not realize, as the reader does, that the kind of prosperity that Animal Farm currently achieves is accomplished in the same way that Jones behaves—that is, at the expense of the animals. Indeed, the deputation of neighboring farmers who tour the farm praises Napoleon for getting greater production while providing less food for his "laborers" than they have been able to do. When the novel ends, the animals are looking in on the festivities between the humans and the pigs, and they find that they can no longer distinguish the pigs from the humans; the transformation is complete. What began as utopia, as heaven on earth, has ended as the opposite of utopia. As Orwell seems to say, good will, good intentions, ideals, common decency are not enough, although they should be. Something in human nature or the human condition prevents man ever from regaining paradise, as it were. Orwell himself would probably not put it this way. He would perhaps echo the famous statement of a noted British lord, Lord Acton: "Power corrupts, and absolute power corrupts absolutely."

CHARACTER ANALYSES

ORWELL'S METHODS OF CHARACTERIZATION

Technically, the point of view used in *Animal Farm* is omniscient. That is, the narrator stands above the action and is able to see everything that happens on the farm and in the countryside around the farm. In addition, the narrator is able to "read the minds" of the characters. However, just because the narrator has these capabilities does not require that he use them, and the narrator of *Animal Farm* does not use all of the capabilities of the omniscient narrator to their full extent.

Thus, although the narrator takes an essentially objective point of view, he tells the story from the general perspective of the common animals on Animal Farm. We never, for example, see how Snowball or Napoleon feels about anything; what the pigs say and do is only reported; nothing more is said about them. We are, however, informed about the general attitudes of the other animals, although only once in the course of the novel does the narrator enter into the mind of one of the animals (he enters Clover's mind to describe her reaction to the purge in Chapter VII). In addition, the narrator does make judgments about the characters, particularly in the early parts of the novel; these judgments are most frequently presented to the reader through the choice of words or phrases, and they should be carefully noted.

These characteristics of the point of view in *Animal Farm* affect the ways in which the reader learns about the characters that "people" the scene and perform the actions. By far the most common source of information about these animals is the description of what they do, both specifically and generally. A second important source of information is through the reports of what these animals say, whether this is presented through direct quotation or through summaries of their statements. Both of these means of characterization are quite objective, and they can lead to different interpretations on the part of the reader. This is one of the reasons that the narrator presents such information from the general perspective of the common animals; the result of this perspective is that the reader *is* biased for these animals and against the pigs. A technique used less frequently than the first two methods of characterization is direct description of the physical characteristics of the animals; in addition, evaluative comments also provide information. Both of these methods help build sympathy for the plight of the common animals and, to a lesser extent, build antipathy against the pigs' takeover of power on Animal Farm.

It should also be noted that the characterization in *Animal Farm* is both flat and static. That is, the characters are given only those characteristics that fit them for a particular role in the scheme of the novel. For example, Boxer is given all the characteristics of a loyal worker; basically, he is only that. Napoleon is a leader, and only that, albeit a very clever one. In addition, once the basic characteristics of each animal have been established, they do not change. Perhaps Boxer is somewhat disillusioned at the end of the novel, but he has the same basic characteristics at the end of the novel that he had at the beginning. Even Napoleon, who brings about the changes that are apparent in the novel, does not basically change; the innovations are simply progressively more blatant manifestations of the characteristics which he displayed at the beginning of the novel. Of course, these progressively restrictive and self-serving manifestations of Napoleon's taste for personal power change the situation in which the animals must exist, but the animals themselves do not change.

Old Major

Old Major is a twelve-year-old Middle White boar. He is a show pig who has won prizes for Jones, who exhibited him under the name Willingdon Beauty. Although his tushes (tusks) are uncut, he has a wise and benevolent appearance, and the animals regard him highly enough to remain awake until Jones goes to bed so they can listen to Old Major speak to them for an hour or so.

In terms of a comparison with the leading figures in the Russian revolution, Old Major is most like Karl Marx, who was the major theoretician behind the Communistic ideals. However, he also has some ideas in common with Lenin. Even if there were no points of comparison between the events in this novel and the events in the 1917 Russian Revolution, though, Old Major would still be an important figure. He is a visionary, a dreamer, who suggests that there could be a better society than the one in which the animals now live.

He feels that the animals are downtrodden and that they could live with more dignity and honor if they were allowed to do so on their own, without being ordered about by the human beings who own them. Indeed, if human beings were eliminated, the animals could enter a new, golden age. The land could, Old Major says, support many more animals in much greater comfort if the animals no longer had to give living space and the fruits of their labors to Man, who is essentially unproductive.

In this new golden age, Old Major envisions the animals not only as having freedom, dignity, and honor, but also as having equality, greater satisfaction, and better health. They can achieve all this, and more, by living simple and natural lives and by avoiding all the vices and even the appurtenances of human beings – alcohol, beds, clothing, and so on. This vision, Old Major's oratorical powers, and the song *Beasts of England* all combine to capture the attention and the imagination of the animals of Manor Farm. Indeed, the animals immediately begin working toward the day when this vision can be turned into reality; after the Rebellion, all of the principles on which Animal Farm will be based are modeled on the ideas in Old Major's speech.

Old Major's vision is just that – a vision. It is, of course, ironic that this vision is developed by a show pig, one who has been pampered most of his life. Far from being one of the downtrodden workers, Old Major has lived a life of ease, spending his days in a stall filled with fresh straw and having all his needs met. On the other hand, this kind of life has allowed Old Major sufficient time to think and also time to observe the other animals. He can formulate such ideas simply because he has the leisure to do so; the other animals have to spend all their time concentrating on hard work and on survival. In Old Major's mind, this golden age will take place sometime in the distant future; it is not something that he believes will happen soon. As a result, his vision is a suggestion of what could be, an outline of a desirable future; it is not a practical plan for how that future can be achieved. In addition, his vision assumes the benevolence and kindness of all animals toward one another, rather than taking into account the actual motivations of individuals. Of course, the purpose of a vision such as this one is to provide a goal toward which a person or a group can work. The details and the steps involved in reaching that goal are foreign to its purpose.

Nevertheless, just as the strength of the first stages of the experiment at Animal Farm rests on the simplicity and the beauty of this vision, so also do the later degeneration and corruption of the ideal rest on that same simplicity.

Snowball

After Old Major's death, just three days after presenting his vision to the animals, Snowball and Napoleon quickly become the leaders in planning for the Rebellion (even though they, too, believe that it will take place at some unspecified future time), and they also take charge of examining and codifying the implications of Old Major's vision. Of the two leaders, Snowball is obviously the one more in sympathy with the spirit of the vision. That is, he organizes committees so that all the animals can take an active part in planning for the Rebellion and in improving life on Animal Farm. He organizes classes in reading and writing so that all the animals can take an informed part in the committee meetings and in the general meetings, as well, so that their lives can be improved. He plans the construction of the windmill as a means to make the lives of the animals more efficient, less difficult, and more comfortable. Indeed, all of the examples of the ideas which he supports, the things that he says, and the activities which he undertakes all indicate that he has captured the spirit and the substance of Old Major's vision.

Snowball complements Old Major. That is, Snowball grasps Old Major's vision, but he also has the practical orientation that is needed to implement this vision in the real world. In terms of the comparison between the action in *Animal Farm* and the events of the Russian Revolution, Snowball plays a role that is, in many ways, similar to the role played by Trotsky. Like Trotsky, Snowball is a planner; he is always looking for ways in which the ideas of Old Major's vision can be made a reality. In addition, he is an excellent orator, able to persuade the animals and able to make them see his side of a question; it is he, for example, who exhorts the animals to perform their work better and more efficiently after the Rebellion has taken place. In addition, he is the primary interpreter of the ways in which the vision applies to practical matters, such as Mollie's concern about being able to have ribbons in her mane. These characteristics also make Snowball an excellent tactician whose battle plan brings victory during the Battle of the Cowshed; his belief in Old Major's vision and in the possibilities it represents are shown by the fact that he is in the forefront of the battle with the humans.

Snowball is not perfect in his adherence to the goals of Old Major's vision—that is, he shares some of Old Major's weaknesses. For example, he agrees with Napoleon that the pigs should have all the apples and all the milk because of the work they do, ignoring the benefits which these foods would have for the other animals. Because Snowball is more active and more talkative, he is thought to have less depth of character than Napoleon has (in actual fact, of course, this means simply that he is more open and less secretive and devious about what he is up to), a belief that contributes to the way in which the animals accept Napoleon's campaign to slander Snowball's character later in the novel. His most serious flaw, however, is that he, like Old Major, does not consider the possibility that others may have other, less desirable goals than he has. He does not, apparently, even consider the idea that his disagreements with Napoleon and his successes in bringing the animals to his side of the arguments might cause Napoleon to act against him. His belief seems to be that any question should be explored fully and that any decision should be made on the basis of a vote by all the animals. He is not always successful in having his position ratified by the vote of the animals, but he does not consider plotting against Napoleon. Consequently, he is not prepared when Napoleon takes action against him, and, as a result, he is chased away from Animal Farm, barely escaping with his life.

Napoleon

Napoleon is a huge Berkshire boar, the only pig of that breed on the farm. He is quite fierce looking, and he often gets his way, even though he does not talk a great deal. Even before the Rebellion takes place, these traits lead the other animals to believe that he has a great depth of character (in contrast to Snowball, who is thought to have a rather shallow character because he is active and talks a great deal).

Napoleon can be both compared and contrasted with Snowball and, to a lesser degree, with Old Major. In essence, Napoleon and Snowball are similar in the ways in which they prepare for the

Rebellion and in which they carry out their goals. They are, on the other hand, very different in the goals that they have and in the ways in which they respond to the situation following the Rebellion. Thus, both Snowball and Napoleon embrace Old Major's vision, and they work to develop Old Major's ideas into a blueprint for a society to be established after the Rebellion. Snowball, of course, envisions plans for the benefit of *all* the animals. In contrast, Napoleon plans the ways in which he can use these ideas for his *own* benefit; it is difficult to say exactly when this goal becomes Napoleon's primary concern, but it is clear that he is working toward this goal just after the Rebellion, when he takes charge of the milk and the apples. Snowball plans activities to help the animals develop; in contrast, Napoleon stays aloof from these activities. He also disagrees with Snowball on most issues. Undoubtedly his stance is a calculated one, preparing for the day when he can eliminate Snowball as a rival; he will then be able to say, with greater authority, that Snowball was wrong all along, that Snowball was working against the best interests of the animals.

Whereas Snowball is a planner who is open and straightforward with his ideas and his plans, Napoleon is a secretive plotter who works behind the scenes rather than overtly. For example, Napoleon trains the guard dogs in secret, keeping them completely hidden from view. He is also good at developing support for his ideas between meetings, when he can talk to each of the animals in private — a situation in which his appearance can intimidate and in which he can adjust his psychological "brainwashing" to each of the animals individually. Until he gains the power he wants, he works steadily to undermine and discredit his opponent, whether by quietly voicing his opposition to Snowball's ideas or by urinating on Snowball's plans for the windmill.

In his maneuvering for power, Napoleon's sense of timing is sure. Enough time has passed since Snowball's bravery and leadership in the Battle for the Cowshed for those acts to be out of the immediate memory of the animals. Napoleon has had enough time to insinuate the idea that Snowball's ideas are not in the best interests of the animals. Thus, he chooses a climactic moment and uses the element of surprise to carry through his plans. Indeed, by the time the animals recover from the shock of Snowball's being attacked by the guard dogs, Napoleon has firmly taken all power and is ready to enforce it.

After his power is absolute, Napoleon displays all the characteristics of a despotic ruler (he shares these traits with Stalin, his counterpart in the Russian Revolution). His main aim is to take more and more privileges for himself and for those around him – the best food, the best quarters, the best produce of the farm, and such luxuries as whiskey, clothing, and fine china. At the same time, he must distract the animals from the fact that the goals of the original vision of Animal Farm are constantly being modified, and he must also disguise the fact that their lives are becoming worse rather than better. He undertakes this task ruthlessly. He introduces the purge, quickly killing those who have opposed him and also killing those who hysterically confess to fictional, alleged crimes. He cuts off the supplies of those who attempt to thwart his will, and he threatens to reduce the rations of those who do not voluntarily work additional hours. He keeps the animals working at laborious projects, such as building and rebuilding the windmill and building the new school, in order to keep them from having the time or the energy to think about what is going on. With the threat of these things in the background, Napoleon's steady propaganda campaign, along with his practice of having the animals give him credit for all the good things that take place, keeps the minds of the animals busy – almost. Napoleon decides that he needs a scapegoat to take the blame for all the failures (he chooses Snowball) and begins putting great emphasis on ceremonies and parades; all of this is very effective in keeping the animals from thinking too seriously about what Napoleon is doing to them.

Napoleon does not change during the course of the novel. One of the first things that the narrator tells the reader about Napoleon is that this pig is used to getting his own way – getting what he wants. This is still his major characteristic at the end of the novel. It is true that, as the novel progresses, Napoleon wants more and more, and it is also true that he, with the help of Squealer, becomes increasingly sophisticated in justifying his increasing greed. Nevertheless, greed is his major continuing characteristic, and at the end of the novel he is still getting exactly what he wants, when he wants it, in the way he wants it.

Squealer

Squealer, next to Napoleon, is the best-known of the other pigs. Even before the Rebellion, he is thought of as being a fine talker, an argumentative sort who can turn an idea inside out and make it seem as though nothing has changed or that the change is clearly superior to the way things were. It is no wonder, then, that he becomes the official propagandist for the pigs after the Rebellion and becomes the official spokesman for Napoleon after his bloodless coup. In the service of his master, Squealer revises history to accommodate whatever Napoleon wants to do, and he also revises the Seven Commandments for the same reason. He also invents the threat of Jones' return as a means of ending all arguments and squelching any prying questions about what he is doing or saying. Squealer does not like to be questioned or to be argued with; for example, he is vindictive about such insubordination, as are the guard dogs, who threaten to attack Boxer after the first purge, and Squealer behaves in a similar way when Boxer only mildly disagrees with Squealer's version of the Battle of the Cowshed and Snowball's role in it. Squealer has no direct counterpart in the Russian Revolution, but every dictatorship and most governments have one or more people who perform exactly the same role that Squealer does; it is their "duty" to interpret the actions of the leader in the best possible way for the purposes of propaganda.

Squealer is a small pig who is very fat. His eyes are bright and apparently merry. Although his voice is high and shrill, he uses it very persuasively, and his persuasiveness is heightened by a peculiar mannerism: despite Squealer's bulk, he is very agile, and he often hops nimbly from side to side, whisking his tail all the while he argues; the more difficult the argument, the faster he hops and whisks his tail.

Boxer

Boxer is the foremost representative of the common animals on Animal Farm; in terms of Marxist theory, he is a representative of the down-trodden working class whose labors go to make others comfortable while he, himself, gains nothing from his work. He has several major characteristics: his size (nearly eighteen hands tall), his great strength (that of two or three ordinary horses), his great willingness to work (he tries to do more and more work throughout the novel, always volunteering for extra work whenever something needs to be done), his steady character (once he accepts something as so, he will not change his mind and he will defend it staunchly), his lack of intelligence (he cannot learn more than four letters of the alphabet, and he has great difficulty reasoning), and his consideration of other animals (when he comes into the barn to hear Old Major's speech, he looks carefully to make sure he does not accidentally step on one of the smaller animals, and he always helps another animal in difficulty when he can). His main trait, however, is his blind, unthinking loyalty to the cause of Animal Farm and his same blind loyalty to its leader. Boxer always attends the farm's meetings, and he is one of the leaders in singing *Beasts of England*. Although he is uneasy about some of the changes taking place, he accepts them, deciding that *whatever* Napoleon says *must* be right. When things go wrong, Boxer does not blame his leader; instead, he believes that the animals themselves must be at fault, and he resolves to work even harder. Indeed, Boxer leads the other workers by his example, working as hard as he can to accomplish the goals of the Rebellion; he works so hard, in fact, that he ruins his health in the service of the ideals expressed by Old Major.

Boxer, of course, stands as an example of the value that the leaders of any totalitarian state put on the individuals within that state. He is of value only as long as he can work hard and lead by example. Of course, however, Boxer is expendable, since Napoleon would have allowed the best worker on the farm to be purged if Boxer's great size and strength were not sufficient to keep the neighbors' dogs at bay. After his useful life is done, the pigs extract the last ounce of value from him by selling him to the glue factory for the money which his carcass will bring. All his hard work and loyalty have gained him nothing, not even a dignified death. Although Boxer never questions what is happening on the farm, and although he never wavers in his faith, he is a tired horse at the end of his life. He has expended so much work for such miniscule results; he must surely realize that something has gone wrong with the dream, but if he does, he never admits it, and he never blames anyone but himself.

Benjamin

Benjamin is the oldest animal on the farm, and he is the worst tempered. He is a survivor. That is, he accepts what he must, all the while believing none of it; he will not take sides on any issue, seeing both sides as unprofitable and not worth arguing about. He believes that neither side is better than the other side and that whichever side comes out ahead, life will go on as usual—badly. He generally keeps his opinions to himself, but when he does express an opinion, he does so cryptically (as we might expect, this leaves the other animals frequently bewildered, but it also protects him against retribution from the pigs). Benjamin works slowly and obstinately, but he does not shirk his duty; on the other hand, he does nothing more than what he absolutely must do. Although Benjamin learns to read as well as any of the pigs, he refuses, on principle, to use his ability, feeling that it is a waste of time from which no good can possibly come. Benjamin is the skeptic, believing that nothing good will come from what is done on Animal Farm, but also believing that nothing good will come of anything else either. Indeed, Benjamin's only "weakness," the only chink in his moral armor, is his unspoken, but steady, devotion to Boxer.

CRITICAL ANALYSIS

THEME

The main thematic emphasis of *Animal Farm* can be stated in several ways: the betrayal of the revolution; the development of a dictatorship; the failure of a bright vision; and the pressure of the status quo on ideas that would change it. Each of these general ideas is accurate enough to serve as the starting point for a discussion of the theme of *Animal Farm*, but it must be recognized that each of these ideas emphasizes only one aspect of the content of the novel while ignoring or diminishing the importance of other aspects. A full examination of the thematic concerns of this novel would include all the ideas listed above, as well as other ideas which are related to them.

Just as the novel itself begins with the presentation of Old Major's vision of what life could be like for all the farm animals, so also should any discussion about the theme of this novel begin with an examination of that vision. Old Major's vision, of course, is a dreamlike outline of what Old Major believes constitutes "the good life." It is popular because it is simple enough for even the least intellectual animals to glimpse. This vision rests on three basic assumptions: man exploits the animals, denying them the fruits of their labors; when man has disappeared, the animals will lead full and comfortable lives because they will have control of what they work to produce; and, by nature, all animals are good and benevolent, while all humans are bad and exploitative. All of these assumptions are simplistic, which leads to their ready acceptance by the animals, but which also leads to the gradual erosion of the animals' ability to control their own destiny.

The idea that man exploits the animals and denies them the fruits of their labors is simplistic for several reasons. The first is that it ignores the fact that someone — whether it be pig or human — must plan and coordinate the activities involved in producing goods of any kind. It may be true that man takes a larger share of the goods produced than his work would actually merit, and he returns less to the animals than they should receive. That, however, is not the question. The question is whether or not any managerial class exploits the animals, since *someone* must make the decisions. The answer that Orwell provides seems to suggest that anyone, whether animal or human, who makes the decisions reserves a primary portion for himself and for others like him.

The idea that the animals will be comfortable and control the fruits of their labors is simplistic in much the same way. Perhaps if the animals had been able to handle the committee system of government, or if they had even been able to think of resolutions to propose for debate and thus to take a full and informed part in their own governance, this idea might have had some chance of becoming a reality. Orwell makes it clear, however, that most of the animals are unwilling or unable to handle such matters; indeed, most of the animals are unable to even make informed choices about the proposals which are presented to them. They do not have the skills to plan their work, and they do not have the skills to plan what they will do with the fruits of their labors; indeed, they do not even have the clarity of mind nor sufficient assertiveness to challenge someone else's decisions about what will happen to them. Under these circumstances, not only is it likely that a managerial class will develop, but it is also likely that the animals will be unable to use the fruits of their labors for their own benefit.

The idea that all animals are equal and that all animals are good and benevolent is simplistic for the same reasons. Perhaps all animals *should* have an equal opportunity and *should* receive an equal share of the goods produced. Nevertheless, all the animals are not able to handle the tasks necessary to the successful operation of the farm. It is possible that they could have been brought to the point at which they could handle the debates and the necessary decisions—if the natural leaders had been willing to take the time and the energy necessary to develop their abilities to that point. However, the belief that all animals are good and benevolent simply does not hold up in practice. Animals have a diversity of personal goals and personal characteristics, and selfishness is one of their characteristics. Unfortunately, those who are selfish, who are out to gain their own personal benefits, frequently displace those who are benevolent and have an abundance of good will. This is certainly the case among the animals of Animal Farm. The weakness of Old Major's vision, however, is that it simply does not take into account, or make any provision for, the diversity found in any group.

Thus, the animals try to work toward making Old Major's vision a reality, but they are simply unequipped to do so effectively. In addition, the simplistic nature of that vision allows uncongenial forces to take over. Because this vision assumes the goodness of all animals, the innocent and trusting have no safeguards against the devious and secretive mind of such an animal as Napoleon, and they likewise have no impetus to be wary of such a person. Because Old Major's vision is broad and general, those animals who wish to use the vision for their *own* personal rewards need only insert the details that move the enterprise slowly toward those ends, gradually modifying even the general outlines of the vision until these outlines reflect a state that is entirely different from the original.

Thus, the dream of a utopian state in which the animals could live in comfort and dignity is corrupted until finally the animals have even less than they had before. Orwell certainly wanted to show how this corruption can take place, and it seems likely that he wanted to do so as a warning, as a guideline so that we could learn what to guard against. In other words, Orwell warns his readers that a vision of a better society *can* be corrupted if care and watchfulness are not exercised; he is *not* suggesting that all visions of a better society *must* necessarily become corrupted. Orwell was a longtime socialist, and although he was offended by the way in which the socialist dream was corrupted in Russia, he still believed that this socialistic dream of his was both viable and desirable as long as the abuses were eliminated.

POINT OF VIEW

Technically speaking, the narrator of *Animal Farm* is omniscient. That is, he knows all of the events which are involved in the rise and decline of Animal Farm, and he knows about all the events occurring in the countryside around Animal Farm. In addition, the narrator of this novel has the ability to "read the minds" of all the characters—human and animal—in the novel. An omniscient narrator always views the action from a point outside that action and slightly "above" it, and the presentation of the action is normally narrated in the third-person point of view.

To say that a narrator is omniscient does not, however, mean that he uses all the abilities that are associated with this point of view. An omniscient narrator can limit what he shows the reader. For example, the fact that the narrator is omniscient and can tell the reader about what each of the animals is thinking is established when he enters the mind of Clover to show her feelings about what has happened to their dream (this occurs in Chapter VII). This is, however, the only time that the narrator directly enters the mind of a single character. At all other times, the narrator restricts himself to presenting the generalized feelings of the animals or to an objective presentation of the events that happen. The narrator further restricts himself to presenting the generalized feelings of only the common farm animals and revealing their perspective in the description of the events. Thus, the narrator presents the pigs strictly from the outside, showing their actions as the common animals would see them.

This point of view is very effective in this novel. The Rebellion and the new state which is to follow the Rebellion is supposed to benefit all the animals. It is supposed to make life better for them and give them dignity. They are enthusiastic about the brotherhood of all animals, and they give their best efforts to planning for the Rebellion. Afterward, they give their best efforts to try to bring the original vision into reality. It is these animals who are betrayed, and Orwell's point of view helps to show not only how the animals are ignorant of this betrayal, but also how they allow themselves to be betrayed.

For the purposes of this novel, it is better that we do not see the motives behind Napoleon's actions. For example, if he sincerely believed that he was doing the right thing, we would have more sympathy for him. Instead, what is important is *what* Napoleon does, not *why* he does it. It is also important that his actions appear to be monstrous, for no matter what his motives might be, his actions *do* betray the revolution, and that is a monstrous thing. Thus, by presenting the events of the novel from the general perspective of the common animals, and by eliminating all narration from the perspective of the pigs, the narrator focuses our attention on the effects of certain key actions – actions which ultimately betray the initial goals of the Rebellion. It is those effects that are important, not the reasons behind the actions that produce them.

The perspective taken by the narrator in *Animal Farm* also has another important advantage: at the same time that the narrator shows the lack of understanding that the animals have about what is happening to them, he also allows the reader to know more than the animals know. For example, when Napoleon takes charge of the puppies, the animals think nothing about it, but the reader suspects that Napoleon is up to something. Another example occurs when the animals find Squealer, after he falls from a ladder, beneath the Commandments painted on the barn. The animals don't understand what he is doing there. They don't associate the changes in the Commandments with the ladder and the bucket of paint; they don't even bother to look up at the Commandments. The reader, of course, is supposed to understand immediately what Squealer has been up to. Thus, the narrator is able to provide the reader with the necessary information to understand exactly what is happening on Animal Farm, while at the same time showing how the animals react and how they let these things happen to them.

The narrative point of view in *Animal Farm* is, then, well chosen. It allows the author to show precisely those things necessary to make his point clear and to avoid dealing with those things that might weaken or obscure that point.

SETTING

The physical setting of a farm is ideal for Orwell's story. It is appropriate to the pastoral, nostalgic vision of Old Major. It also has the necessary isolation from the world for the birth and development of a new society. Its life is simple in the sense that it is unlike the urban life typical of the twentieth century.

The setting is ideal in another way. Because it is pleasant and pastoral, it offers the most vivid possible contrast to the direction which the society of Animal Farm will take—that is, the setting will be inappropriate to the authoritarian society of Napoleon. This is shown especially well in the scene on the knoll after the purge trials, when Clover looks upon the attractive landscape and wonders what has gone wrong while the animals have tried to put Old Major's vision into practice. It is almost impossible for her to believe that in such a place bloodshed and cruelty—man's inhumanity for man, in effect—could become a part of day-to-day life.

That the story should be set in England, like *Nineteen Eighty-Four*, is significant. Orwell was never mysterious when he had something to say to his fellow man. As in the later novel, he is saying: it could happen *here*.

STORY

In prose fiction, the term *story* refers to the chronological-causal sequence of events. In the story itself, the first event is the one that happens the earliest in time. The next event arises out of (or is caused by) the previous event and follows it in time. This continues until the last event of the novel, which arises out of the sequence of events before it and follows those events in time.

Every novel has a story, a chronological-causal sequence of events. In some novels, however, the events are not presented to the reader in the order in which they happen. The story in *Animal Farm* is presented directly and in a straightforward manner. Old Major's speech, in which he presents his vision of a better future is the first event presented to the reader, and it is the first event to happen in time; it provides the impetus for all of the later actions in the novel. The party during which the pigs and the humans become indistinguishable is the last event to happen in time, as well as the last event presented to the reader; it is the culmination of all the things that have happened before it. All of the events between the first and the last events march in a steady progression in time, each one leading into the next.

Orwell's purpose in this novel is to show the reader the rise of Animal Farm in Old Major's bright vision and how and why its fall occurs under Napoleon; he leads us from Old Major's vision to the drunken brawl in which the pigs and the humans are indistinguishable. To do this, Orwell uses graphic scenes plus narrative passages to move the story along, and as in conventional novels, he foreshadows later actions. The combinations of a fairly straightforward story line and a plausible characterization of the animals – partly human but still sufficiently animal – are certainly two major reasons why the novel has such a direct impact on the reader.

PLOT

The term *plot* refers to the way in which the events of the story are presented to the reader. The most obvious examples of plot in novels are found in those that present the story events in their chronological-causal sequence. There are, however, other elements involved in the construction of plot than simply arranging and rearranging the story events. For example, developing the story so that the events are constructed with a rising action, reaching a high point, and then following this with a falling sequence from there, thus balancing one event against another; here is evidence of the author's careful concern for the way in which the reader receives the necessary information that comprises *Animal Farm*.

Originally developed to describe the way in which drama develops, the following sequence of parts describes the structure of *Animal Farm* (and of many other stories and novels): exposition; inciting incident; rising action; climax; falling action (denouement); and conclusion. In this scheme, the climax is the high point of the story – the emotional peak or the point at which the action begins to decline in some way. The climax marks the point at which the rising action ends and the falling action begins.

There is very little direct and separate exposition in *Animal Farm*; the background information that is required to set the scene and the situation is presented in the first two paragraphs, with all other details woven into the description of the inciting incident and into the rising action. The essence of the exposition is, of course, that Jones drinks more than he should and that he does not manage his farm well, often leaving the animals underfed and uncomfortable.

The inciting incident is Old Major's speech in which he tells the animals his thoughts about the opposition between humans and animals; he tells them of his vision of a better life after all humans have left England. This speech starts the animals thinking about how their lives could improve and stirs them to begin planning for a Rebellion to take place in some unspecified future. It also prepares us for the actual Rebellion after Jones and his men try to beat the hungry animals away from the food they need. In short, this speech—the inciting incident—puts into motion the train of events that culminates in the pigs becoming indistinguishable from the humans.

The first climax of *Animal Farm* concerns the expulsion of Snowball from the farm. Until this happens, there is hope that the animals will be able to improve their lives and control their own destinies. After this happens, everything seems to go downhill for the common animals. The conditions under which they live become increasingly harsh, and they progressively lose what freedom they had. Thus, the expulsion of Snowball is the event that marks the turn in the direction of the events in the novel; it is an emotional high point as well.

The rising action—imagine, for example, the gradual upward slope of a hill—begins with Jones firing the shotgun and ends with Napoleon ordering his dogs to attack Snowball during Snowball's impassioned speech in favor of the windmill. It includes such things as the planning which the animals do for the three months following Old Major's speech, the failure of Jones and his men to feed the animals, the uprising when Jones and his men try to beat the animals away from the food, and the animals' victory gallop around the farm, culminating in their tour of the farmhouse, changing the name

from Manor Farm to Animal Farm, and painting the Commandments on the barn wall; in addition, there is the first—very successful—harvest, the committee meetings, the Battle of the Cowshed,
the defection of Mollie, and the debate over the feasibility of
building a windmill.

The falling action begins when Napoleon mounts the raised
platform and announces that, henceforth, pigs will decide what work
will be done around the farm and how it will be done; instead of
wasting time in useless debates, the Sunday meetings will be used
to give orders for what *must* be done. If the rising action can be
likened to the top of the hill, the falling action, or denouement, as it
is sometimes called, can be compared to the downward slope on the
other side of the hill. In this novel, the falling action includes such
actions as the building (and rebuilding) of the windmill, the trade
with humans, the pigs moving into the house and assuming other
"human" privileges, the purge, the changing of the Commandments,
the Battle of the Windmill, the pigs' first alcoholic binge, the death
of Boxer, and the pigs beginning to walk on their hind legs.

A conclusion brings something to a close; it wraps up something at a logical point. The party that the pigs give for the neighboring farmers provides the conclusion for *Animal Farm*, for it is
this event that rounds off what was begun by Old Major's speech.
The animals were first seen living under a human being who drank
too much and who treated the animals badly. As this final party
shows, the animals are ultimately dominated by pigs who are indistinguishable from human beings, who drink too much, and who
treat them badly. The situation of the animals on Animal Farm has
come full circle, and there is no logical need to continue the story of
their struggles any longer.

Earlier, it was suggested that the action of a story can be compared to a hill, with the rising action paralleling the upward slope,
the climax being the top of the hill, and the falling action being the
downward slope on the other side. This is a useful image for most
novels, for they usually end at a point at least somewhat different
from the point at which they began. For *Animal Farm*, however, it
might help to think of the novel's construction in terms of a circle,
for the conditions of the animals at the beginning of the novel and at
the end are so similar as to be indistinguishable. Thus, the beginning
point of the novel, as well as the ending point, would be at the very

bottom of a circle standing on edge. The climax would be at the very top of this circle; in point of fact, the climactic event in *Animal Farm* is described just a page or two short of the exact center of the novel, emphasizing the symmetry of the rise and fall of the ideal of free animals controlling their own lives.

Other elements in the novel also stress the symmetry of the structure and of the theme. Characters are balanced against one another and yet, at the same time, they are paired with one another. Snowball, for example, is contrasted with Napoleon, and yet they are, for a time, two halves of the leadership team; later, black is turned to white, and vice versa, as Snowball is metamorphosed into the "villain" and Napoleon is metamorphosed into the saving "hero." Boxer, the true believer and ever-ready volunteer, is contrasted with Benjamin, the eternal skeptic who does only what he must do in order to survive; nevertheless, they are comfortable companions. Like the characters, scenes are also balanced against one another. For example, the Battle of the Cowshed is balanced against the Battle of the Windmill, with the latter battle showing how things have changed since the earlier battle. The prediction that, when he is through with his useful life, men would sell Boxer to the glue factory is balanced by the fact that the pigs, who have become much like men, do indeed sell Boxer to the glue factory. The scene in which the Seven Commandments are painted on the barn wall is balanced by several scenes in which the animals discover that, one by one, the Commandments have been modified or changed, until only one original Commandment is left. The drunkenness of Jones in the very first paragraphs of the novel is balanced by the drunkenness of the pigs and the humans in the very last paragraphs of the novel. Each of the human activities that Old Major inveighs against are gradually adopted by Napoleon and his porcine elite. Other character groupings and other balanced scenes further contribute to the balanced and symmetrical structure of *Animal Farm*.

Although *Animal Farm*'s story is presented in a straightforward and uncomplicated way, its plot is carefully worked out. It is the plot of the novel that is involved in the symmetry of the rising and the falling action, and it is the plot of the novel that is involved in the balancing of characters and of scenes. The presentation of the situation and of the events that occur has been worked out carefully to achieve the greatest possible clarity and the greatest possible impact. That is the function of plot.

LITERARY CONVENTIONS AND DEVICES

Like any novel, *Animal Farm* makes use of a number of literary conventions and devices, and some of these are worthy of particular note. For instance, the novel is a modern example of a *beast fable*; that is, the characters are, for the most part, animals, and the story is about what happens to these animals. *Satire* is involved, since part of the purpose of using animals as the characters is to ridicule certain human traits and activities. *Utopia* and *dystopia* are terms used respectively to describe a perfect society and a society gone wrong; Old Major's vision describes a utopia, while the actual society in the last half of the novel is a dystopia. *Irony* refers to certain kinds of reversals of expectations and to certain situations in which the reader knows more than the characters know. Finally, *symbols* are often objects that stand for some idea or some other object; for example, the American bald eagle and our national flag are symbols of the United States. Each of these symbolic devices and conventions is important in the development of *Animal Farm*.

The beast fable is a form that is used to remove a sequence of actions from the day-to-day world so that we can see it in some kind of perspective that we might not otherwise find. In this particular case, the beast fable allows us to view the rise and fall of a change in society with some detachment, to see more clearly what happens to the social ideal and how it fails. If the characters had been human beings, a greater emphasis would have been placed on the characters themselves, and the reader's reactions would have focused on the human emotions, rather than on the forces and activities involved in the failure.

To be successful, a beast fable must capture the right balance between human characteristics and animal characteristics in its portrait of the animals. The animals must be human enough so that we can see that the situation does apply to human beings and so that we can recognize the animals as at least vaguely representative of types of human beings. On the other hand, if the animals are not sufficiently animal-like in their characteristics, there is no point in using animals as the characters. Orwell is successful in finding this balance; his animals have just enough human characteristics to serve his purpose and to make them recognizable as human types, but most of their characteristics are those of a particular type of animal. For example, Boxer is a loyal, hardworking, and rather unintelligent horse. Coupled with his size (nearly eighteen hands tall), these are characteristics which one might well imagine a horse to have—if a horse could talk and had a personality. In other words, the character traits which Boxer is given are human traits, but they are also consistent with the kind of animal he is. The pigs, of course, become increasingly human, but that is part of the theme of the novel; they do move, however, from animals with a *few* human traits to almost literal "humans" with a number of animal traits.

Both satire and irony are achieved through the beast fable. In a horse such as Boxer, we admire his traits of loyalty, his hard work, and his single-minded sense of purpose; that he lacks intelligence makes little difference to us. However, if we think of human beings who show the same kind of single-minded, unthinking loyalty to a leader, we are not as admiring; indeed, we should realize that this kind of reaction is a major factor in allowing Napoleon to do whatever he wants to do with Animal Farm. In this way, Orwell keenly satirizes human beings and their methods of dealing with social change and with social responsibilities. Even though Boxer remains a horse throughout the novel, he also represents a certain human response to situations and problems; the comparison does not flatter the human who responds in the ways in which Boxer responds. Irony is also developed through the nature of the characters. The major irony in *Animal Farm* is the way in which the pigs turn into human beings. This is a reversal of expectations, for the pigs were supposed to lead the animals into the "brave new world" of Old Major's vision; instead, they led the unsuspecting animals into a world in which the animals were eventually worse off than they were before. Even though one of the novel's climactic scenes has been prepared for, the scene in which the pigs parade around the yard on their hind legs is a shock. Another facet of this same irony is that the reader knows more about what is happening than do the animals to which it is happening. Thus, the reader at least suspects that Napoleon is up to no good when he takes over the education of the puppies, while the animals suspect nothing. The reader knows why Squealer is lying on the ground with a bucket of paint, but the animals never do seem to figure out that he has been responsible for changing the Commandments painted on the barn. Indeed, the reader understands each of the new actions that the pigs instigate better than the animals do, providing the reader with an ironic insight into the situation on Animal Farm and with a clearer perspective about the nature of political manipulation.

Situational irony involves the reversal of expectations in a scene, a situation, or even in an entire novel. Dramatic irony involves situations in which the audience knows more than the characters; it is especially involved in situations in which the characters believe that things will be improved or take a turn for the better, while the audience knows that they will take a turn for the worse. The movement from a utopian vision to dystopian reality in this novel is also an ironic reversal. Old Major's vision is a dream of a perfect world in which man has been eliminated, in which all animals are well-fed and comfortable, in which all animals are equal to one another. The animals begin to work toward the goal proposed by the dream, and they are enthusiastic about it. Indeed, their initial enthusiasm and the brightness of the vision keeps them plodding along even when the vision begins to slip away from them. The reader, of course, can see in every new chapter how Animal Farm is moving away from that ideal, how precious rights and privileges are being abused. The reader can see the situation becoming steadily more dystopian as the pigs take more and more power and privilege into their own hands and give less and less thought to the animals. The reader can see, and understand, how miserable the situation has become for the animals, while the animals themselves feel only a vague sense of loss and hopelessness. The utopian vision that begins the novel and the dystopian reality that ends it are diametrically opposed, adding yet another dimension to the irony and the satire of the novel.

The symbols in the novel function as guidelines for the reader and are indications of the animals' beliefs and feelings. For example, *Beasts of England* is a symbol of the hope and the enthusiasm with which the animals respond to Old Major's vision; for the reader, Napoleon's prohibition of the singing of this song is a clear indication that Napoleon is eliminating a possible point of comparison with what is actually happening. The whip is another symbol, first of the cruelty of Jones and his men and, later, of the fact that the pigs have become nearly human in their actions and in their ideas. The windmill is another two-sided symbol; at first, it symbolizes the hope that the animals have for a better life on Animal Farm; later, it becomes a symbol of the mindless, backbreaking work and drudgery to which the animals are subjected in order to leave them with little time for thinking about their original goal. The farmhouse, the name of the farm, the Commandments on the barn, the knacker's wagon,

Mollie's ribbons – these, and many other points, arise out of the life of the animals and take on significance because of the emotional and intellectual value which they are given in the course of the action; thus, they become symbols of the animals' feelings and of the significant ideas, values, and events in the rise and fall of Animal Farm. Through devices such as those discussed above, Orwell enriches and clarifies the themes of *Animal Farm*, guides the reader's perception of the events that occur, and enhances the reader's enjoyment of the work. Although *Animal Farm* may seem to be a simple little story, an awareness of the patterned structure and of the conventions and literary devices that have been used to develop and shape the story indicate that it is a very carefully crafted novel with greater depths than are at first apparent.

STYLE

Orwell's style shows the same simple, self-conscious honesty as his own personality. He never stoops to obscure complexity to achieve effects; indeed, he never uses effects for their own sake. His two main goals in writing were to communicate his political lessons and to achieve an effective literary style; and the simpler and clearer his style, the more effective his lesson. For this reason the language of *Animal Farm* is simple and unadorned, and the story is expressed in a straightforward and logical way. Orwell does not write "purple passages"; he prefers the effect of understatement; the tone is always carefully controlled.

Orwell is particularly good at two things: selecting the exact detail to describe daily life – as, for example, the way in which Boxer and Clover are shown to walk into the barn in Chapter I; and, later, embodying political ideas in such a way as to reveal their truth or falsity – as, for example, the use of the Commandments and the way they are altered.

QUESTIONS FOR REVIEW

1. Analyze the way in which Orwell depicts Napoleon's career in the novel in relation to the well-known quotation: "Power corrupts, and absolute power corrupts absolutely."

2. Suppose the point of view of the novel were Napoleon's. What effect would the reader's seeing everything through Napoleon's eyes have on the novel as it now stands? In what ways would it be a different story?

3. Select a short passage from the novel to illustrate Orwell's use of point of view. Explain in detail how the passage gives evidence of this particular point of view.

4. Why couldn't this novel have been set in London? There would be dogs and cats, at least, to make up the citizenry of Animal Farm.

5. Analyze the scene of the Battle of the Windmill (Chapter VII). How does it begin, and what is the turning point in the fight? How do the animals react to their victory? In other words, explore the dramatic means which Orwell uses to present the scene.

6. Examine the scene of Napoleon's trial and executions (Chapter VII). According to the way in which the scene is presented, why do the animals confess? Why does Napoleon want these confessions? What does this scene demonstrate about the psychology of dictators?

7. Contrast Snowball and Napoleon specifically on their qualities for leadership. How do the animals respond to each, and why is each animal's response different?

8. Contrast Clover and Mollie. How do they differ in personality? What does each represent in the story?

9. For what reason did Orwell include the character of Benjamin? What view of life or of society, or both, does he represent?

10. Collect all the details describing the style of living which Napoleon adopts as leader of Animal Farm. For what reasons

does he assume this style? What relationship does it have to his political beliefs?

11. Justify the idea that Napoleon's banishing of Snowball is the turning point in the plot of the novel and, hence, is important in describing its structure.

12. Would it have been possible for Orwell to show the pigs becoming human at the end of the novel without bringing in actual human beings? Defend the presence of human beings here.

13. Catalogue all the meanings which the windmill has when it is used as a symbol. At any point in the novel, does it ever represent more than one meaning simultaneously? If so, point out where.

14. Compare *Beasts of England* with the new song which Minimus writes, as well as the poem which he composes in Napoleon's honor. What changes do you notice, and of what significance are they in relation to events in the novel?

15. Assemble details which obviously refer to characteristic aspects of Russian society; the decorations given and the naming of battles are two examples. Find as many others as you can.

16. Explain why Napoleon constantly uses Snowball as a scapegoat. Indeed, why is it necessary for Napoleon to have a scapegoat at all?

17. Analyze Squealer's speeches to the animals as propaganda. What means does he use to convince them that Napoleon is always right no matter what he does? How sound is the logic of Squealer's arguments?

18. In Orwell's satire of a totalitarian society, what role do Napoleon's dogs play? How does he use them to control the animals?

19. Explain the relationship between the alteration of Commandments Four and Five and the actions of the pigs? Why do they

bother to have Squealer change the way the Commandments are stated on the wall of the barn?

20. Explain the alteration of the last Commandment. Exactly what does the new version mean?

SELECTED BIBLIOGRAPHY

ATKINS, JOHN A. *George Orwell: A Literary and Biographical Study.* New York, 1955. A book which emphasizes Orwell's ideas and the relationship of his life to his writing.

BRANDER, LAURENCE. *George Orwell.* New York, 1954. A critical study which considers "only those writings which have appeared in book form."

HOLLIS, CHRISTOPHER. *A Study of George Orwell: The Man and His Works.* Chicago, 1956. A book which "criticizes his writings and his ideas" and includes some biography.

REES, RICHARD. *George Orwell: Fugitive from the Camp of Victory.* Carbondale, Ill., 1962. A study of Orwell's writing, plus a personal memoir.

VOORHEES, RICHARD J. *The Paradox of George Orwell.* Lafayette, Ind., 1961. A study of "certain lines of paradox which run through Orwell's life and writing."

WOODCOCK, GEORGE. *The Crystal Spirit: A Study of George Orwell.* Boston, 1966. Another recent study of Orwell's writing which attempts to explain his ideas in a biographical context.

NOTES

Your Guides to Successful Test Preparation.

Cliffs Test Preparation Guides

Efficient preparation means better test scores. Go with the experts and use **Cliffs Test Preparation Guides.** They'll help you reach your goals because they're: Complete • Concise • Functional • In-depth. They are focused on helping you know what to expect from each test. The test-taking techniques have been proven in classroom programs nationwide.

Recommended for individual use or as a part of formal test preparation programs.

TITLES		QTY.
2068-8	ENHANCED ACT ($5.95)	
2069-6	CBEST ($8.95)	
2055-6	CLAST ($8.95)	
2071-8	ELM Review ($8.95)	
2060-2	GMAT ($7.95)	
2064-5	GRE ($9.95)	
2066-1	LSAT ($9.95)	
2046-7	MAT ($12.95)	
2033-5	MATH Review for Standardized Tests ($8.95)	
2020-3	Memory Power for Exams ($4.95)	
2017-3	NTE Core Battery ($14.95)	
2044-0	Police Sergeant Examination Preparation Guide ($9.95)	
2045-9	Postal Examinations ($10.95)	
2032-7	PPST ($7.95)	
2074-2	SAT I ($9.95)	
2042-4	TASP ($8.95)	
2024-6	TOEFL w/cassette ($14.95)	
2007-6	Advanced Practice for TOEFL w/cassettes ($19.95)	
2034-3	VERBAL Review for Standardized Tests ($7.95)	
2043-2	WPE ($8.95)	
2041-6	You Can Pass the GED ($9.95)	

Prices subject to change without notice.

Available at your local bookseller or order by sending the coupon with payment to:
Cliffs Notes, Inc., P.O. Box 80728, Lincoln, NE 68501.

❏ Money Order ❏ Check made payable to Cliffs Notes, Inc. ❏ VISA® ❏ MasterCard®

Card Number _____

Expiration Date _____

Signature _____

Name _____

Address _____

City _____

State _____ Zip _____

Cliffs® NOTES INC.

P.O. Box 80728, Lincoln, NE 68501

Legends In Their Own Time

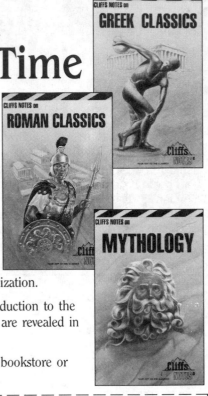

Ancient civilization is rich with the acts of legendary figures and events. Here are three classic reference books that will help you understand the legends, myths and facts surrounding the dawn of civilization.

Cliffs Notes on Greek Classics and *Cliffs Notes on Roman Classics—* Guides to the ideology, philosophy and literary influence of ancient civilization.

*Cliffs Notes on Mythology—*An introduction to the study of various civilizations as they are revealed in myths and legends.

Find these legendary books at your bookstore or order them using the attached form.

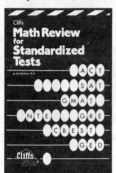

Think Quick...Again

Now there are more Cliffs Quick Review titles, providing help with more introductory level courses. Use Quick Reviews to increase your understanding of fundamental principles in a given subject, as well as to prepare for quizzes, midterms and finals.

Think quick with new Cliffs Quick Review titles. You'll find them at your bookstore or by returning the attached order form.

Do better in the classroom, and on papers and tests with Cliffs Quick Reviews.

Cliffs NOTES ®. INC.